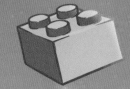

CONTENTS

WELCOME TO LEGO® CITY!

A tourist got off the train at LEGO City station. It's going to be his first visit to this town full of bricks! Have a close look at the rest of the passengers sitting in the window seats and find the characters from the box below among them.

TIME FOR A SNACK

Lead our tourist to the snack shop – he needs fuel if he wants to tour the entire city!

START

FINISH

PHOTOS FROM THE TRIP

Have a close look at the pictures the tourist took and find 8 differences between them. When you spot a difference, colour in one of the heads at the bottom of the page.

Look at the 8 smaller photos and find them in the picture above.

WHO WILL WIN THE TROPHY?

The tourist is checking out a local race. Add up the numbers on each track to find out who won. The driver with the highest score will take first place and win the trophy!

1
3
4

3
1
3

3
3
1
2

2
4

=

=

=

SURPRISE!

Connect the dots to see what surprised the tourist so much.

AN EVER-CHANGING CITY

Find out which building the crew is pulling down today.
Look at the pieces the builders are thinking about.
They come from the buildings that will stay intact.

Just one demolition vehicle might not be enough. Draw one more!

FOSSIL DATING

TO THE RESCUE

There's been an accident in the mountains! Fortunately, the helicopter has already transported the unlucky tourist to the hospital. Look at the 6 smaller photos in the box on the right and find them in the main picture.

Look at the doctor in the helicopter pilot's thought bubble and find him in the picture. He will take care of the injured tourist.

A BUS RIDE THROUGH TOWN

Sightseeing in LEGO City? The best way is to take the awesome tour bus! Match the missing vehicle pieces from the box below with the empty spaces and write the correct number in each space.

Now look at the photos above and mark the one that the tourist took from the bus.

ICE CREAM TO GO

Count each type of ice cream in the tourist's thought bubble and write the numbers in the box on the right. The ice cream that appeared the least is the one the tourist picked in the end!

RAFTING TRIP

Navigate the tourist and his guide through the stream, following the sequence below. Watch out for drifting logs and rocks jutting out of the water!

START

KEY

FINISH

LEGO CITY

ON THE TRAIL

Look closely at what is happening on the beautiful LEGO City mountainside and use the grid system to answer the tourist's questions. Find the objects from the box below in the picture.

A

I

2

3

4

5

DO YOU KNOW:
1. ON WHICH TWO SQUARES YOU CAN SEE BIRDS?
2. ON WHICH SQUARES YOU CAN SEE TOURISTS IN HELMETS?
3. WHERE THE LOST BINOCULARS ARE?
4. ON WHICH SQUARE YOU CAN MEET A BEAR?

1
B1   D1

2
A5   C2

E1

E3   F3

3   **4**
E5   A4

B   C   D   E   F

CATCH THE CROOK!

The tourist is witnessing some police action. Help the officers catch the crook. Connect the dots to make the net appear.

WHICH WAY TO TOWN?

The tourist got lost and stumbled upon a mining site. Help him find the way back to town by following the worker's instructions. Watch out for spiders!

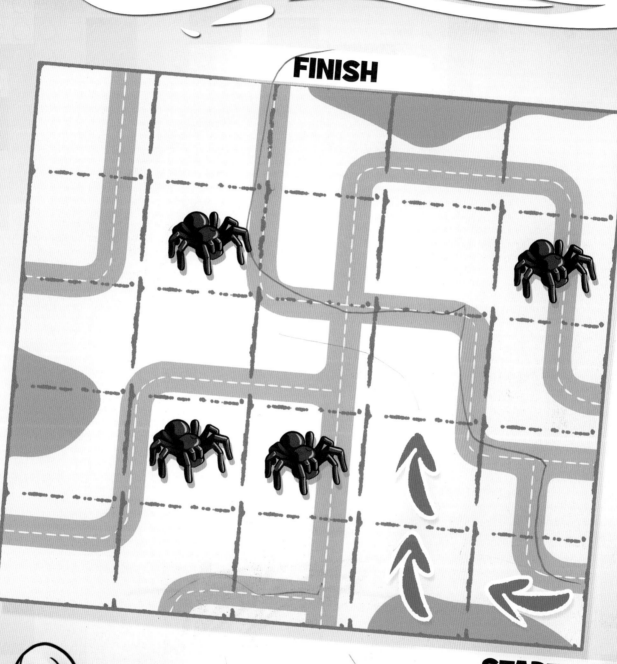

FINISH

START

SPEED RECORD

"Stop! Thief!" cries the police officer. A crook just robbed the LEGO City bank!

"You'll never catch me, copper!" shouts the crook.

"We'll see about that!" says the police officer. "You'd be surprised what can happen!"

Down the street, an ice cream vendor starts her busy day. "Ice cream, ice cream!" she shouts. "Get your cold, refreshing ice cream!"

A sweaty tourist sees the ice cream vendor. His mouth starts watering. "Boy, I could really go for some ice cream!" he says.

Meanwhile, the chase continues! The crook thinks he's getting away.

"Ha!" laughs the crook, looking behind him.

But the crook doesn't see the ice cream truck just ahead. Or the ice cream vendor!

"Whoa, what's that?" says the ice cream vendor.

"Hit the brakes!" yells the ice cream vendor. "You're going to –"

CRASH!

The red sports car runs right into the ice cream truck. Bricks fly everywhere!

The crook and the ice cream vendor soar through the air.

"Noooo! My money! Grab the money!" shouts the crook.

"Noooo! My ice cream! Grab the ice cream!" shouts the ice cream vendor.

But what about the bricks? They're heading straight for the tourist!

The bricks land right next to the tourist and piece together. A few seconds later, there's a table with an umbrella, and a couple of seats, too.

"What luck!" says the tourist, sitting down. Then suddenly ... PLOP! PLOP!

Two ice cream cones land in his hand!

"You want sprinkles with those?" asks the ice cream vendor.

"Well, a small café like this seems like a good idea, doesn't it?" the ice cream vendor ponders. "I always wanted to spend more time in one place."

"Just like this crook who will be spending more time in jail," the police officer replies.

"Aw! There are no sprinkles in jail!" the crook says, being led to the police car.

The End!

A SURFBOARD FOR THE CHAMP

The Pro Surfer needs a new cool surfboard.
Design one for him!

1

2

IS A BIT HARD TO HUG. `4`

WON'T SAY NO TO A GOOD WEB. `2`

CAN BE VERY FUNNY. `3`

LOVES FAST CARS. `1`

3

4

WHO'S WHO?

Connect the descriptions with the characters by writing the correct number in each box.

BATTLE DWARF ATTACKS!

The Battle Dwarf punched a hole through the wall. Which of the four holes did he make?

x13

SCARY MICE

The Elephant Costume Girl is really afraid of mice. Count the mice she's dreaming about and write the number in the box.

HANDS FULL

Help the Gourmet Chef collect all the dishes so they can be distributed amongst the restaurant guests. You can't take the same path twice and you can only pick up each dish once. Be careful not to step on a banana peel!

START ➡

FINISH

Draw lines to connect the pairs of objects that go together.

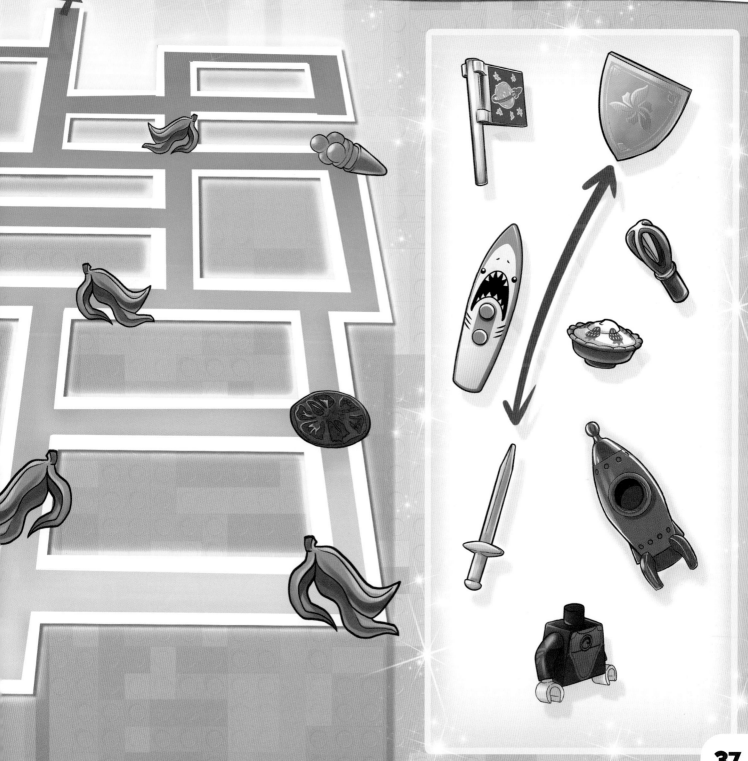

37

AT THE OTHER END OF THE LASSO

Find out whose birthday it is by following the Cowboy Costume Guy's lasso.

ELF MAIDEN'S SHIELDS

Which shield is identical to the one the Elf Maiden is holding?

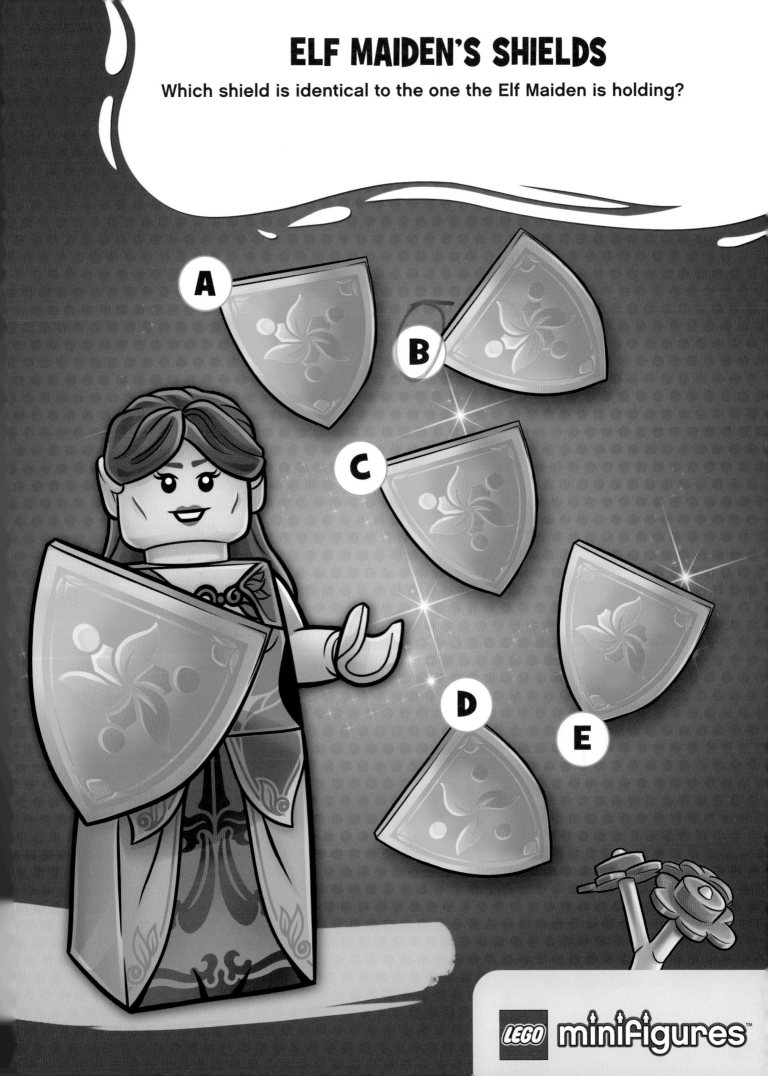

HEY, WHERE'S MY PET?

Which of the animals is Connoisseur's pet?

ACTOR NEEDED

Which character should be placed in the box with the question mark to complete the pattern? When you find that out you'll know what kind of actor the film director is looking for.

WONDER WEAPON

FLOWERPOT GIRL

Look at the scattered puzzle pieces from Flowerpot Girl's picture. Match them with the empty spaces.

MYSTERY MAN

What mood is the Mystery Man in today? Draw an expression on his face for every day of the week!

Monday

Tuesday

Wednesday

Thursday

Friday

Saturday

Sunday

LEGO minifigures™

MAGICAL TREE

Colour in the other half of the tree so that the flowers and fruit are the same on both sides.

LET'S DANCE!

The Dance Instructor is maxing out! Look at the dance routines and complete them by writing the correct letters in the boxes.

SPACE JOURNEY

Guide Rocket Boy through the arrow labyrinth so that he reaches his planet.

START

FINISH

Draw an expression on
Rocket Boy's face according
to the descriptions below.

1 After meeting a cosmic octopus.

2 After hearing a galactic joke.

3 After finding his planet.

49

LOST ITEMS

Connect the lost items with their owners.

CREATURE TRACKER

Retro Space Hero is looking for strange cosmic beings.
Draw the creature that left these tracks.

WHO'S MISSING HERE?

Find and circle the character who is missing from the group photo.

CARNIVAL SUDOKU

Can you finish this sudoku? Remember that the carnival party guests should appear only once in every row and column.

53

BALLOON IDEAS

The Party Clown is going to a birthday party, but he only knows how to make a dog from a balloon. Connect the dots in the speech bubbles to show him what else he can make!

LEGO minifigures™

TWIN RODEO

Lots of cowboys came to this year's rodeo. Look at the participant at the top and find his twin brother.

A QUEUE AT THE VET'S

Who is first in line to see the Veterinarian? Colour the picture according to the key to find out who she is waiting for.

LEGEND

| 1 | 2 | 3 | 4 | 5 |

WHERE ARE MY DOUGHNUTS?

Help the children find rectangles with these two sequences of doughnuts. They appear only once in the big picture.

LEGO minifigures™

ANSWERS

p. 6–7

p. 8

p. 10–11

p. 12

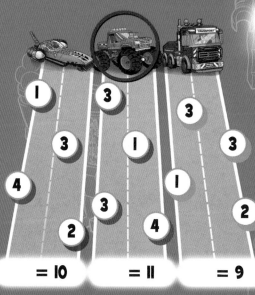

= 10   = 11   = 9

p. 13

p. 14–15

p. 18–19

p. 20-21

3 2 1 5 4 D

p. 22

6 2 4 3

p. 23

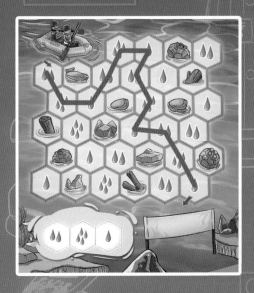

p. 24-25

1 B1 D1
2 A5 C2
   E1
   E3 F3
3 E5 4 A4

p. 27

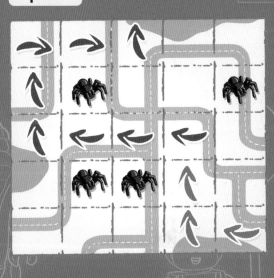

p. 33

IS A BIT HARD TO HUG.	4
WON'T SAY NO TO A GOOD WEB.	2
LOVES FAST CARS.	1
CAN BE VERY FUNNY.	3

p. 34

p. 35

x 13

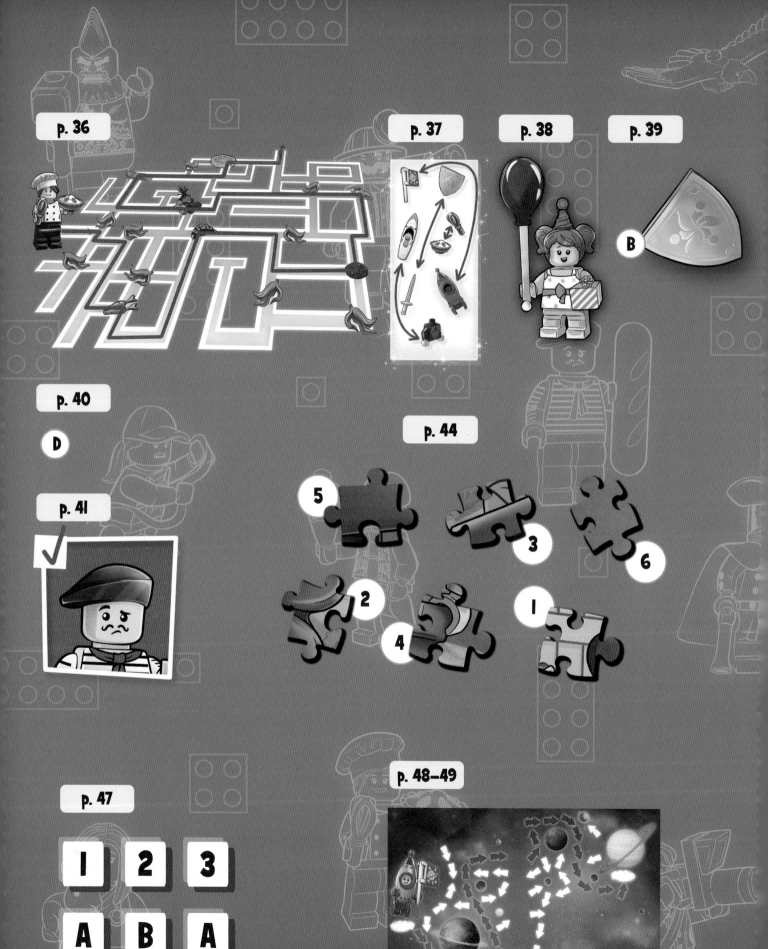

p. 36

p. 37

p. 38

p. 39

B

p. 40

D

p. 44

5

3

6

p. 41

✓

2

4

1

p. 47

1 2 3

A B A

p. 48–49

p. 50

5

1

2

100 100

4

3

p. 52

p. 53

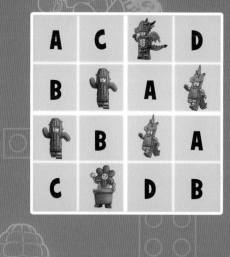

A	C		D
B		A	
	B		A
C		D	B

p. 54

p. 55

5

p. 56

p. 57

BUILD YOUR OWN MINIFIGURE

Use your LEGO pieces and follow the steps shown to build your own minifigure.